PRAYERS FROM THE CLOISTER

Deepening friendship with God

DOM ALAN REES

First published in 1996 by
KEVIN MAYHEW LTD
Rattlesden
Bury St Edmunds
Suffolk IP30 0SZ

ISBN 0 86209 881 5
Catalogue No 1500067

Cover photograph: Tim Rawle
Design and artwork by Veronica Ward
and Graham Johnstone

Typesetting by Louise Hill
Printed and bound in Great Britain

CONTENTS

FOREWORD

'Lord, teach us to pray.' These words of the
disciples of Jesus are on the lips of many
people today. We want to pray but all too
often we do not know where to begin. We can
identify so easily with the words of St Paul:
'We do not know how to pray as we ought'
(Romans 8:26); and we can make the mistake
of thinking that prayer happens just through our
own effort. Indeed, prayer does involve effort,
but again, as Paul says, 'The Spirit helps us in
our weakness . . .' and we need the Spirit of
Jesus to lead us in our prayer. Our halting words
of praise, petition and confession, made in the
Holy Spirit, are joined to the prayer of the Lord
Jesus, who offers them on our behalf to the
Eternal Father.

In prayer, we deepen our friendship with
God; we can approach him with confidence
because he loves us as his own. Everything we
do, everything we are matters to him. Prayer is
not separate from daily life; it is within the
chaos of our daily living that true prayer is
born, because it is there that we meet God
and know our need of his love.

A number of the prayers in this collection were born out of the need to express in prayer the problems and challenges presented by daily life. Others came as a result of meditating on the Gospels in the age-old monastic practice of *Lectio Divina* (Holy Reading). This form of prayer is a meditative approach to the Word of God where we read a few verses, absorb them in the silence and listen and respond to what God might be saying to us at that moment. Hopefully, the Gospel prayers will encourage those who use this book to try this ancient form of prayer in *Lectio Divina*.

May this book help its readers to deepen their friendship with God through prayer.

DOM ALAN REES
BELMONT ABBEY, HEREFORD

Gospel Prayers

*Zacchaeus, hurry and come down; for I must
stay at your house today.* Luke 19:5

Often, Lord, we are unable to see you   *1*
   because we are like Zacchaeus,
   short of stature –
   not physical, but spiritual stature.
We are so blinded by our prejudices,
   by our pride, our comfortable life.
We may not be wealthy,
   but we all possess so many things
   that keep us from seeing you clearly
   in our lives.
The house of our life is full
   to overflowing with trivia.
Yet, Lord, you are able to see us;
   your gaze can pierce the trivia
   and touch a heart that wants
   a glimpse of you.
You came to make your home with us,
   and you will not be satisfied
   until you have made your home
   in the heart of each one of us.
Seek me out, Lord, call to me,

bid me come out of my hiding place
and welcome you into my home.
Sit at my table, eat with me,
    listen to my story, have pity on me
    and forgive my preoccupation
    with the trivialities of life
    which prevent me from coming to you.
Bring salvation to my house
    and my heart will rejoice.

God be merciful to me a sinner. Luke 18:13

*Let us, then, have no fear in approaching the
throne of grace to receive mercy and to find grace
when we are in need of help.* Hebrews 4:16

When I come before you in prayer   2
   I am very much aware of your holiness
   and of my own unworthiness.
Yet you have come to seek
   and save what is lost,
   to raise up sinners
   and to heal the broken-hearted.
Your love yearns for me,
   your compassion reaches out to me,
   your mercy urges me to have
   boundless confidence.
Let your love take away my fears;
   let your compassion enfold me
   and let your mercy fill me
   with a deep sense of being forgiven
   and held in the everlasting arms.

> *He prostrated himself at Jesus' feet*
> *and thanked him.* Luke 17:16

> *Let us give thanks to the Lord our God . . .*
> *it is right to give him thanks and praise.*

3 Lord, we are very good at asking you
    for things.
In our many needs, we come before you
    on our knees imploring your help.
Like the ten lepers, we cry out to you,
'Jesus, Master, have mercy on us!'
Yet, when you grant our requests
    and we go our way rejoicing,
    how often do we come before you
    with the same urgency in our thanksgiving
    that went into our request?

We are so selfish and forgetful, Lord.
Forgive us for treating you
    in this discourteous way.
We are so ready to complain to you
    when things don't go our way,
    but how often are we found
    prostrate at your feet,
    thanking you for the

many and wonderful blessings
that follow us through life?

When we lift our hands in praise
and our hearts in thanksgiving,
we try to give you the whole of our attention,
the whole of our heart;
we try to centre on you the source
of all life,
of all good,
of all blessings.
Help us, dear Lord,
to be a people with grateful hearts
who live only for the praise
of your glory.

*A woman named Martha welcomed him into her
home. She had a sister named Mary who sat at the
Lord's feet and listened to him.* Luke 10:38-39

*They urged him strongly: Stay with us, because it
is almost evening and the day is nearly over.
So he went in to stay with them.* Luke 24

*. . . we will come to them and make our
home with them.* John 14:22

*Listen, I am standing at the door knocking; if you
hear my voice and open the door, I will come to you
and eat with you, and you with me.* Revelation 3

4 Lord, you love to be invited
        into our home –
        into the house of our heart.
    Whatever the poverty of the dwelling,
        you love to be made welcome.
    You pitched your tent
        in the midst of a sinful people;
    you made your home in our flesh.
    You came and sat at our table,
        carried our burdens,
        walked with us along our weary way.

You love to be with us where we are –
   in bright and sparkling homes,
   in dirty and sordid homes,
   in homes where there is no love
   or compassion,
   in homes cheerful with kindness and care,
   in homes grey with misery,
   darkened by depression and
   uncomprehended bereavement.
You are always waiting to come in.
You never force an entry –
there is no insistence,
   because you are filled with the
   divine courtesy that never presumes
   on a person's freedom.

Come in, Lord.
I open to you the door of my heart.
I am often reluctant to invite you in
   because I am ashamed of what is inside.
You know too what is there,
   but you do not mind,
   because your concern
   is to put everything in order
   through gentleness and love.
Teach me to be like these two sisters:

like Martha, in opening the door to you
   and welcoming you;
like Mary, in being attentive to your word,
   because therein is my life.
You can do without me fussing around you,
   attending to unimportant things.
What you really want
   is the attention of my heart,
   fixed on you in love.
You are not content with
   scratching the surface of my life.
You are a God who is satisfied
   only with my all.
I invite you into my life
   to take my all
   and to be my All.

*But while he was still far off, his father saw him
and was filled with compassion.* Luke 15:20

The most heartening and comforting thought 5
that comes to me when I read the parable of
the Prodigal Son is that the father never left
the son. He carried him in his heart all through
his wandering and carousing and sin. The son
wandered off from the father's house, he cut
family ties and didn't want to know – but the
father held him on that cord of love.

God can never cut that eternal cord which
comes from his heart. We can try to break it,
snap it, tear it, cut it – but it refuses all our
strength. We can only ignore it, hide from it,
avoid it – but it is still there and at that
moment when we are most desperate we will
seek it and find strength in it.

O Love that wilt not let me go . . .
I rest my weary soul in thee.

How often I have walked
    out of your house, beloved Father,
    rich with the bounty of your grace,
    and squandered it.
How I could have despaired

had I not known the parable
of the prodigal Son.

In the midst of my sin
and despair, Lord,
your love has reached out to me
and brought me home.

How can I face my father,
how can I tell him what I have done?

I rehearse my piece
but you don't want to hear it.

You enclose me in your arms,
your eyes look at me with love eternal.

You order your servants
to restore to me the robe of grace
and you seat me at the banqueting table
to feast on that
to which I have no right, but which,
in the generosity of your love,
you give me.

You do not stand on your dignity,
you do not lecture me on justice –
you embrace me,
your eyes show compassion,
you restore me to yourself
and make me live again.

The Christian faith is about being restored to life – God's life; God's life is his love. 'I have come that you may have life and have it to the full.' The church exists to bring this life to young and old. When the angel released the apostles from prison (Acts 5:19) he told them to go and tell the people the whole message about this LIFE. The story of the prodigal son shows us how the Father wants to restore us to life and love.

Lord, I pray for the ministers of the church.
Let them always remember this parable.
Let them remember that they too
   are sinners brought to life by Jesus,
   and on them has been laid
   the privilege and responsibility
   of bringing others to Life.
Sadly, there have been times
   when the people have not experienced
   life at the hands
   of the church's ministers.
Have mercy, Lord,
   for this failure to impart the life
   that you have promised in abundance
   to your people.
Let the church's ministers

be filled with compassion;
let their gaze reflect the love
   in the eyes of Jesus for the sinner.
May they always remember
   that they are channels of God's mercy,
   and to him alone belongs any judgement.

Lord, he whom you love is sick. John 11

The sisters of Lazarus sent news   6
   of his illness to you, Lord.
They trusted you to do what was best.
You didn't rush to them;
you allowed Lazarus to die
   before you set out.
You knew what you were doing.

So often, we come to you
   with our requests
   on behalf of the sick and suffering.
We spend hours telling you
   what you should do for them.
I know this is a sign of our concern
   for our loved ones who suffer,
   but, Lord, in the end,
   it is only you
   who know what is best for them.

Teach us how to bring the needs
   of the sick and dying to you
   in faith, hope and confidence.
Teach us to lay these needs before you
   humbly and simply,
   believing that your healing touch

will reach out to them
and that your love and mercy
will surround and support them
in their time of need.
Teach us that your purposes
will always be fulfilled
and your name be glorified
the more we put our trust in you.
In you, Lord, we put our trust.
Let us never be put to shame.

*Didn't I tell you, if you believe you will
see the glory of God.* John 11:40

Lord, take away the stone   7
    from the entrance to my heart.
Let out the stench of corruption,
    decay and death
    that has been there so long;
let the new person emerge,
    no longer bound by past sins
    but unbound and made free
    by your healing love.

Take off the grave clothes and let him go!

MEDITATION AT THE FOOT OF THE CROSS

FATHER, FORGIVE THEM, FOR THEY
KNOW NOT WHAT THEY DO

*Forgive us our trespasses as we forgive those
who trespass against us.* Matthew 6:12

8 Jesus dies as he lived – at the moment of his greatest suffering, as the nails were piercing his hands and feet, as the burning pain of the wounds inflicted at his scourging sears his body, as his head throbs through the wounds made by long, sharp thorns, as his heart is broken in love for a world that has sinned, is sinning and will sin, he is able to utter what God alone can utter – the word of forgiveness, which sets the seal on all his love.

Lord Jesus, we feel
   that we are hard done by –
   victims of unfairness,
we have been harshly treated
   or abused by people,
we feel deeply hurt in so many ways.

It is hard to forgive –
    we are so bound by our resentment,
    by our hatred.
We call ourselves Christian –
    followers of Christ,
    yet we are so slow to imitate
    our Lord and Master
    in this area of forgiveness.
You gave us the example of service:
    'If I, your Lord and Master,
    have washed your feet,
    so ought you to wash one another's feet.'
You knelt before your friends
    with a bowl of water and a towel
    in an act of loving service,
    even though you knew
    that before that night was past
    they would betray you,
    deny you
    and forsake you.

Now on the cross,
    you forgive your murderers.
Your eyes turn towards us
    because we too are your murderers.

Your eyes are full of love
    and forgiveness –

and also they are full of
unspoken appeal:
Will you also forgive?

In a moment of silence, let us bring into our
hearts all those whom we cannot forgive for some
reason or another. Let us pray for them, and for
ourselves, that God will give us the power
to forgive as he has forgiven us.

TODAY YOU SHALL BE WITH ME
IN PARADISE

Not long ago, Lord,   *9*
   you stood on the mountain of Transfiguration,
   flanked by Moses and Elijah
   who had confirmed you
   in your divine mission.
Here is the end of that mission –
   to be lifted high on the hill of Calvary
   flanked by the sin of humanity –
   thieves, robbers, scoffers, mockers.
You, Lord Jesus, entered into our
   human condition –
   you came into our very depths,
   the sinless one was made sin
   for our sake.

He came to his own and his own people received
him not, but as many as received him he gave
power to become children of God.

Here, on Calvary, we see that take place. The
criminal who scoffs sums up all those who do
not believe in Christ; he joins himself with
the officers of the law who jeer, 'If you be the

son of God, come down from the cross; save yourself'. There is no faith.

But there is another side to the cross. The good thief – who owns his sin and sees your innocence. In that moment, he comes to salvation – in the acknowledgement of sin, he receives forgiveness and the assurance of eternal life. He comes to faith – and in faith is glory.

I have come to call sinners, not the righteous.

We know our sin – we acknowledge it . . . or do we? On which side of the cross do we find ourselves? Are our hearts prostrate before the innocence of Jesus weighed down with our sin, or are we faithless and self-satisfied, blaming God and the world for everything?

In a moment of silence, let us take our place
at the side of Jesus on the cross.

WOMAN, BEHOLD YOUR SON . . .

And a sword will pierce through your own soul too.

When Mary said 'Yes' to God at the *10*
Annunciation, she could hardly have known
the extent of the suffering that she would
endure. She would have known the scriptures
that the Messiah would be the Man of
Sorrows, and now at this moment of deep
grief she becomes the Mother of Sorrows. Her
heart is at one with the Sacred Heart of Jesus
in suffering for the sin of the world.

At that moment
   of your deepest pain, Lord Jesus,
   your only concern is for your mother;
you commit her to the care
   of your dear friend,
   who takes her into his own home.
At that moment, Lord,
   you gave us into the hands
   of your mother –
   you also gave her into our hands.

The Church has always loved and cherished
Mary because she is the mother of our
Redeemer – she shared in that great work by

which we are made sons and daughters of the
Father. As she shared in her son's sufferings
on the cross, so she continues to share in the
sufferings of the Church his Body, and she
will continue to do so until the end of time.

Mary, you will always be there for us
    the Mother of Sorrows
    and Mother in our sorrow.
Pray that in our sufferings
    we may always stand at the cross
    with you, the Mother of Jesus
    and our Mother, who comforts us
    in all our distress.

*In silence now let us bring to her the pain of so
many of her children on this earth at this moment –
those who suffer the pain of war, violence, inner
distress, incurable sickness, and so many other
wounds of body and spirit.*

My God, my God, why have you forsaken me?

In the Incarnation, Jesus entered the very *11* depths of human distress. We experience that distress when we feel rejected, forsaken, totally alone, bereft of consolation, near to despair – even at the very point of despair. This cry of Jesus on the cross shows us that he is there with us. Anything of mental or spiritual anguish that we suffer cannot match the agony of Jesus at that moment. This is the point when he was most united with our pain – it was the moment of the greatest self-emptying.

Lord Jesus, whenever we feel most lost,
    rejected,
    deserted,
    we must believe that you have been
    in the deepest chamber of darkness
    that the human soul can experience.
Being the perfect human being
    you could experience
    only the very height, depth and breadth
    of human suffering.
You have been there,
    so let us remember

that you will take our hand
when we are in the hell of despair
and will lead us out of the darkness.

In silence, let us make an act of faith in
God's presence in the many moments of darkness
of our lives, and pray that he will
always lift us out of them.

I THIRST

If anyone is thirsty, let him come to me and drink.
As scripture says, out of his heart shall
flow rivers of living water.

In your suffering, Lord Jesus,   *12*
    you thirsted.
They gave you vinegar to drink,
    and some drugged wine to ease your pain
    but you wouldn't taste it.
Your deepest thirst was for
    the salvation of the world.
As when the disciples urged you to eat
    at the well in Samaria, you replied,
'I have food to eat
    of which you do not know'.
So now, you thirst as Saviour
    for our souls and for our salvation.
And it is of the chalice
    of God's loving purpose to save the world
    that you are now drinking.

And you invite us
    to taste of that chalice;
    out of that chalice –
    your heart broken in love for us –

flows blood and water,
rivers of living water –
the Holy Spirit of love.
It is for this purpose that you have come
so that we should drink
of that overflowing love of your Spirit.
We eat the bread and drink the cup
of the love of God at that family table
to which we have been invited
as sons and daughters,
reconciled and forgiven.

*In the silence, we ask to experience that same
desire for the salvation of others that was in
that cry of the Lord: 'I thirst'.*

IT IS FINISHED

Thirty-three short years are over. When we *13*
hear of the sudden or tragic death of a young
person, we are saddened by the loss of a life
that has not reached the fullness of years. But
the fullness of years is not in quantity but in
quality, in achievement, in completion.

Your work, Lord Jesus, is complete;
you have done what the Father
    had given you to do –
'Having loved his own
    who were in the world,
    he loved them to the end.'
Your work was to love,
    even to death on the cross.
You could do no more –
    through the cross you have brought together
    heaven and earth;
the gap has been closed.
'God loved the world so much
    that he gave his only Son;
whoever believes in him shall not perish
    but have eternal life.'
The earthly giving is complete
    but God's love is eternal,

everlasting, unending –
'of his fullness we have all received',
   and will continue to receive
   as long as we approach with open hands
   and loving hearts.

*In silence, we immerse ourselves in the eternal gift
of God's love, and pray for those who have not
yet realised his generosity or whose eyes are
not yet opened in faith.*

FATHER, INTO YOUR HANDS
I COMMIT MY SPIRIT

We came from God, and we can be sure that *14*
we shall return to God. We cannot avoid death.
There are two moments of which we can be
sure – the moment that is *now* and the moment
we shall die. 'Pray for us, sinners, now and at the
hour of our death' – these are the two points of
reality for each of us.

The past is gone, we leave it to God's mercy;
the future is uncertain, we give it to God's
providence. But we live *now*, and we ask for
God's help to live this moment as he wants us
to, so that we can be ready at the moment of our
death to meet him, and to hear his resurrection
greeting: 'Peace be with you' – Shalom.

Help us to put into your hands, Lord Jesus,
    each successive moment of our lives.
Every day our prayer has to be
    your last prayer on the cross:
'Father, into your hands
    I commit my spirit.'
Show us how to make this great act
    of faith, of trust, of surrender;
help us to tell our heavenly Father

that we trust him absolutely
    and entrust everything we are, and have,
    and hope to be into his care.
You told us 'do not be anxious;
    look at the birds of the air;
    they neither sow nor reap
    nor gather into barns,
    and yet your heavenly Father feeds them.
Are you not of more value than they?'

Let us always believe that our God is a God
who cares because he loves. We may go
through the valley of darkness, but he is there
with us – he is our shepherd who goes before
us. He has plumbed the depth of our darkness
so that he can take us to the heights of his joy.

In the silence, he asks us: Will you trust me?
Will you surrender your life to me? Will you
believe that I want only what is best for you?
I look at you with the eyes of my Son, the eyes of
Jesus, that are full of tenderness, love, mercy and
forgiveness. Believe that, and say, 'Father,
into your hands I commit my spirit'.

EASTER PRAYERS

*When it was evening on that day, the first day of
the week, and the doors of the house where the
disciples had met were locked for fear of the Jews,
Jesus came and stood among them and said,
'Peace be with you'.* John 20:19

Lord, by your cross and resurrection,   *15*
  you have broken through every barrier.
Neither stone, nor wood,
  nor the hardness of the human heart,
  nor the darkness of death
  could hold you from bursting forth
  into the freedom of the life of the Trinity
  and taking us with you.
It is the one desire of your heart
  that we should experience this freedom –
  the freedom of your risen life,
  the freedom of the truth
    that comes from your Spirit,
  the freedom of the road to eternity:
  the freedom of Jesus,
    our way, our truth and our life.
Nothing can keep us from this if we seek you
  with sincere, loving and faithful hearts.

Like Mary Magdalen, we might seek you
   with our eyes misted with tears of grief;
   like Thomas we might seek you
   through our doubts;
like the disciples we might be
   locked up in the fear of our hearts
   and our search might have come
   to a full stop.
You will not allow these barriers
   to keep us from you,
   because for our sake
   you have sanctified yourself,
   so that we may be sanctified in the truth.
And you have told us that the truth
   will make us free.

Lord, we desire to experience
   this freedom – freedom from fear,
   freedom from doubt, freedom from grief.
Lead us into all truth
   by the power of the Spirit which you,
   our Risen Lord and Saviour,
   lovingly pour upon us,
   and let the whole world resound
   with the new song of your joy –
   Alleluia.

Christ is the beginning, the head of the Church;
where he has gone, we hope to follow.
Mass of the Ascension

Risen Lord Jesus,   *16*
   you have burst asunder
   the bonds of death,
   you have gone beyond the limitations
   of our human existence.
You have promised to come back for us,
   so that where you are we may be also –
   in the place you have prepared for us.

Implant in us, Lord, a deeper hope
   and a more urgent longing
   to be with you in that place of joy
   that knows no end.
Fill us with the desire to transcend
   the confines of our human aspirations
   and to fix our hearts
   where true joy is to be found –
   at home with you in the happiness
   of eternal peace and love.

*. . . When the Spirit of truth comes he will lead
you to the complete truth . . .*   John 16:13

*Indeed you love truth in the heart, then in the
secret of my heart teach me wisdom.*   Psalm 51

*If you make my word your home you will indeed be
my disciples; you will come to know the truth,
and the truth will set you free.*   John 8:31

17   Lord, when you stood before Pilate,
           he asked you, 'Truth, what is that?'
     You, the Truth, stood before him
           yet he failed to understand.
     We too, Lord, often fail to see
           the true meaning of the situations
           in which we find ourselves.

     Before you gave yourself up to death,
           you told us that you are the Truth,
           and that you would send your Spirit
           to lead us into the complete truth.
     You prayed that we would be
           sanctified in the truth.

     Without your Spirit
           we cannot know the truth;

left to ourselves, we remain deluded,
   darkened in mind and heart –
   only partly living.
All the promises that you have made
   show that you want us to be fully alive.
'I have come that you may have life
   and have it to the full.'
We are alive when we come into your truth.

Sadly, too often I prefer to remain
   in my darkness, my illusion,
   afraid to open myself to your truth.
But herein is wholeness,
   so why, Lord, am I so reluctant
   to experience the healing
   that you are waiting to give
   when I enter into the greater reality
   of your life?
What fear holds me back
   from that gentle yet all powerful love
   that is in your heart?

In the secret of my heart,
   teach me the wisdom
   that comes from the Spirit of Truth.
Purify my heart
   of all those hidden things within

that cling to the darkness and shadows
of this finite world,
and let me be open
to the greater possibilities
of life with you.

Let me not be deluded
by the deceitful whisperings
of so many voices
that would hide the truth from me
and from those who seek you.

Let me always admit my truth –
even though this might sometimes
cause me pain.

It is only when I am prepared
to admit the truth about myself
that I can be prepared to enter
into the fullness of truth which is you.

In prayer and in the reading of your Word,
I open myself to the Truth.

Here I can be at home with you,
and in the safety of your presence
I can show you who I am –
honestly and openly.

And your Truth will touch my truth,
and I will find freedom and healing.

King of Glory, Lord of hosts, leave us not orphans.
Send upon us the Promise of the Father,
the Spirit of Truth. Alleluia.
Liturgy of the Hours

GENERAL PRAYERS

EVERYDAY PRAYERS

18 Lord, open my mind to seek you;
my eyes to behold you;
my heart to love you,
and in loving you
may I love all those
made in your image and likeness.

19 Lord,
I pray for all those
whose lives have touched mine,
for good or evil,
in the past or in the present,
whether they are alive or departed.
Give them an abundance
of your grace in this world,
and in eternity
may they find joy in your presence,
in the name of Jesus the Lord.

A Prayer of Invocation

Holy Spirit, Lord and giver of life, be present. *20*
    In my weakness, be my strength;
    in my tiredness, be my freshness;
    in my dirtiness, be my cleansing;
    in my blindness, be my vision;
    in my coldness, be my fervour;
    in my meanness, be my generosity;
    in my hard-heartedness, be my
      gentle compassion;
    in my stupidity, be my clarity;
    in my arrogance, be my humility;
    in my complexity, be my simplicity;
    in my anxiety, be my peace;
    in my hurt, be my healing;
    in my suffering, be my consolation;
    in my troubles, be my calm;
    in my doubts and despondency,
      be my hope;
    in my sin, be my forgiveness,
      mercy and salvation;
for the sake of Jesus
    and the glory of the Father.

A Prayer for Grace

21 Lord, for today,
I simply pray that I may love and be loved;
that I may serve as you served;
that I may give myself for my brothers
and sisters.
Today, I pray that I may share your word
in the power of the Spirit
as opportunity presents itself,
and that I may never be held back
by human respect or fear.
Give me the spirit of prayer
and of continued thanksgiving
in all circumstances of life,
especially in the difficult ones.
Heal me, Lord,
and grant me simplicity and unity
within myself,
through Jesus Christ the Lord.

Prayers of Hope and Truth

Into your hands, heavenly Father,   *22*
    I place this new day.
You know how wayward I am;
    you know how quickly my thoughts stray
    from you and from Jesus,
    the way, the truth and the life.
I ask you to give me your Holy Spirit
    in good measure this day;
    may he be my guide.
May he govern every detail of my life,
    however small and insignificant.
May he fill me with love and praise,
    so that every moment of this day
    may belong to you.
Without you, O holy and blessed Trinity,
    my life lacks purpose,
    but filled with the gift of the Holy Spirit
    it takes on the dimension of your glory.
Stay with me, great God,
    and enable me to live for the praise
    of your glory.
I ask this in Jesus' name.

23   Lord Jesus Christ, Saviour and Redeemer,
I ask you to be Lord of my sleep;
    be Lord of my resting and of my rising;
    be Lord of my dreams.
Do not let the evil one approach me
    in the hours of my sleep.
Breathe the gentle breath of the Holy Spirit
    into my heart during these hours of
    unconsciousness;
        even while I sleep let him be my teacher
        and guide.
Speak your word to my heart
    – words of peace and consolation.
Lift me up into the Father's arms,
    way above the cares and anxieties,
    the temptations and sufferings of this life;
    way above the snares and deceits of the devil.
Let me rest surrounded by the Father's love,
    secure in the salvation won for me
    by your precious blood,
    and abiding in the resurrection joy
    through the power of the Holy Spirit.
I make this prayer in your name, Jesus,
    for to you, together with the eternal Father
    and the life-giving Spirit, belong all power,
    glory, might, majesty and praise. Amen. Alleluia.

Father, make me realise more and more   *24*
    that it is only in being stripped of everything
    that I am more given to you;
    and when I am more given to you,
    then am I truly free.
Let me cling to nothing;
    let me lose all to gain all.
Let me never rely on myself;
    when I cannot cope
    let me hand everything over to you
    and just trust you,
    remembering that I am your child
    and you care for me.
Let me accept humiliation and the cross
    with Jesus crucified.
Let me remain hidden and humble
    in union with your Son.
Let me always remember
    that the only thing that matters
    is to be totally united with your will
    and in this is my peace.
Let my prayer be always Amen! Alleluia!

PRAYERS OF REPENTANCE
AND FORGIVENESS

25   Lord Jesus, heal me of the wounds of yesterday
        that I may live abundantly today
and with confidence in your Providence
        go forward into tomorrow.

26   O Holy Spirit of God,
        cleanse my eyes to see as you see;
        cleanse my ears to hear you speaking to me;
        cleanse my lips to speak only your words;
        cleanse my mind to discern clearly
        what is from you;
        cleanse my heart and fill it with your love,
        love that will overflow to all your people;
        cleanse my body
        and make it more and more your temple;
to the glory and praise of the Father.

Heavenly Father, I confess my sins to you: *27*
 the sins of the past and of the present;
 those hidden and forgotten
 as well as those remembered;
 my sins of thought and desire,
 of word, of deed and of omission;
 the sins that I am too dull of heart to see;
 the sins that others can see and I cannot;
 the sins known to you alone.
I am sorry for all of them.

I ask you to forgive me
 through the merit of Jesus, my Saviour.
Please renew your life in me
 by the power of the Holy Spirit.

Lord, forgive me my sins: *28*
 my lack of faith,
 my lack of hope,
 my lack of love.
I look to you,
 kind and gracious God.
My heart is open.
Please give me
Faith, Hope and Love.

PRAYERS OF FAITH AND COMMITMENT

29 Thank you, Lord, for this new day.
Thank you for the people
   you will put in my way:
   people wounded by life,
   by sin, by others;
   broken people created by you for love
   but not experiencing it.

Thank you for them.
Let me never add to their burden,
   to their grief.

Use me for them,
   if only in a smile
   and an encouraging word
   to bring them life and light.

Let me live in the truth today, Lord;
   let your truth become my truth
   and please set me free in the process.
Let me abide in you and let your word,
   your will, become my home.

30

All I ask, Lord, is that
   your glory may shine forth in this place.

All I ask is that
   you give us what is best for us all
   and for each one.

All I ask is that
   we may love you and each other personally
   and with our whole heart.

Help me to surrender all my vain wishes,
   anxieties and desires
   and give all things into your waiting hands.
Grant me the faith and trust
   that accepts everything from you as a grace,
   a blessing and an opportunity for growth.
If this causes pain, let me accept it
   and understand it as a
   transforming experience.
Help me not to put obstacles
   in the way of your will,
   nor to give in to sadness and anxiety
   when there is darkness and conflict in my life.

31 Lord Jesus, lead me, give me the spirit of prayer.
Teach me to pray, as you taught your apostles;
   give me courage to go with you
   into the lonely mountains
   and pray to the Father in the secret of my heart.
Teach me to struggle in prayer
   as you struggled in the garden of Gethsemane.
Draw me closer to yourself and to the Father
   through the Holy Spirit.
Help me to overcome all obstacles,
   and teach me not to be afraid
   when I have to face certain things
     within myself
   which seem to be more than I can cope with.
Help me in naked faith to go on
   knowing that you are there,
   calling me and drawing me,
   even when all seems dark and arid.
Give me the strength of the Spirit
   to overcome my fear.
Deepen my friendship with you;
   although I am not worthy of such a gift,
   I know that you want me to have it,
   so I take heart and come to you
     confidently,
   trusting in the promises you have made.

Father, you have always been there,   *32*
   even from my earliest years,
   gently leading me on.
Just as you were present
   in the time of the Exodus,
   a pillar of cloud by day
   and a pillar of fire by night,
   leading the Hebrew people
   out of bondage into freedom,
   so it is with me.
You have always been there, Lord,
   leading me out of darkness
   into your wonderful light;
   from ignorance into truth;
   from the isolation of self
   into the community of love.

Despite my wanderings,
   despite my complaining,
   despite my unwillingness to go forward,
   you have never deserted me.
You have always remained faithful
   in the midst of my infidelity.

In the daytime of my joy,
   your hidden brightness,

the wisdom of the Holy Spirit,
   has gone before me and drawn me after it;
in the night-time of my isolation,
   despondency and fear,
   your pillar of fire,
   the refining Spirit,
   has been there working in my heart,
   thawing my iciness and purifying me.
Who can resist you, great God,
   ever seeking after us
   and compelling us to run
   to the light of your truth
   and the warmth of your love?

But, Father, pilgrim that I am,
   I still wander into the byways of pride,
   self-pity and fear.
I take my eyes off the goal all too often,
I allow my weariness to lessen my response
   to your infinite love.
Forgive me as I turn my eyes back to you.
Sharpen my awareness of your Son,
   Jesus, my brother,
   who takes me by the hand
   and pulls me along in my reluctance.
Too often have I looked back over my shoulder,

forgetful of your infinite desire to lead me on
to the glory that lies ahead.

Lord God, how thankful I am
  that you are continually searching for me;
  how thankful I am
  that your grace prompts me to recognise you
  and to give myself to you
  even in my imperfect way.
Lord Jesus, how thankful I am
  that your love,
  stronger than death,
  will never let me go.
Holy Spirit, sweep me up into this love
  which unites you and the Father and the Son;
  let it flow into me
  and overflow from me to all whom I meet.
Let it lighten their darkness
  and increase their joy.
Let it draw me into unity with my brethren
  and with all those whom I serve
  and will serve in your name
  until the end of my days.

Glory and praise to you,
Father, Son and Holy Spirit, for ever.

33 I unite and submit my will to yours
in every event of this day
however unpleasant,
happy or boring.
I will try not to be cast down by blame,
failure, weakness and loneliness,
nor elated by praise and success.
Keep my soul in peace with you, Lord,
and my body relaxed and free of tension.

A Prayer in Time of Trouble

Lord, I acknowledge my utter helplessness   *34*
  in this situation
  and my total dependence upon you.
I bring this problem to you with confidence,
  knowing that all things are possible with you.
Turn it to a means of good, not evil,
  for those involved,
  and by your love take the bitterness
  out of any painful circumstances
  or relationships,
  so that everything may be healed,
  reconciled and resolved through your power.

PRAYER TO MARY

35 Mary, I come before you,
　　imploring the love and care
　　of your most pure and motherly heart.
Look upon us,
　　your frail and sinful children,
　　with pity and concern.
Enfold us in the love of your heart –
　　see us only in the love of your Son
　　who died for us.
Turn us to him with all our hearts.
Remember the fervent and the wayward,
　　those who do not or who cannot pray,
　　the sick in mind, heart and body,
　　those who are unfaithful to your Son
　　in their lack of love and zeal.
Love us and care for us;
　　keep us close to you
　　and your Beloved Son
By your prayers, may we be converted
　　and brought to repentance
　　and newness of life.
Pray for me that I may see myself
　　as I truly am;
　　help me to turn more completely

to my Saviour,
deepen my life of prayer,
take away fear and increase love.
I bring before you
those who have asked my prayers,
those for whom I should pray,
who need prayer,
especially my family,
my friends and benefactors,
and those who depend on me in any way
for help and guidance.
Enfold them in your heart
and bring them to Jesus.
Have pity on the sufferings
of all people,
convert the sinful,
help all come to know the Lord.
Grant peace and hope
to this troubled world.
Amen.

PRAYER IN THE SLIPPER
CHAPEL, WALSINGHAM

36 God our Father,
    you sent the Holy Spirit on Mary
    and she conceived and gave birth
    to Jesus your Son.
O wondrous mystery!
Send the Spirit on me
    that Jesus may be born daily in me.
May I always contemplate the mystery
    of his presence within;
may I give him to the world.
May Mary, in her divine Motherhood,
    teach me how to contemplate
    and participate in this mystery of love.
Purify me by the fire of the Spirit
    that Jesus may find in me
    a worthy dwelling place,
    and that I may have eyes only for him,
    a heart fixed on him
    and a life filled with his glory.

Prayers of Blessing
and Commendation

I surrender myself totally to you, Lord.   *37*
I renounce my own will and desires.
I accept the cross with praise and thanksgiving.
I will not fight you, Lord,
    nor the difficult people and circumstances
    that come my way.
I renounce all rebellion
    and place myself at the disposal
    of my brothers and sisters
    in trust and serenity.
I surrender myself totally to you, my Lord.

38 May the Mind of Jesus
         renew my mind.
     May the Wisdom of Jesus
         enlighten my thoughts.
     May the Words of Jesus
         be in my ears and on my lips.
     May the Heart of Jesus
         beat with my heart.
     May the Cross of Jesus
         be my strength.
     May the Forgiveness of Jesus
         free me from sin.
     May the Healing of Jesus
         bring me to wholeness.
     May the Peace of Jesus
         still all my fears.
     May the Love of Jesus
         fill my whole being.
     May the Risen Jesus enrich me
         with joy, hope and new life.